Wild World

Watching Lions in Africa

Louise and Richard Spilsbury

 **www.heinemann.co.uk/library**
Visit our website to find out more information about Heinemann Library books.

To order:

 Phone 44 (0) 1865 888066

 Send a fax to 44 (0) 1865 314091

 Visit the Heinemann Bookshop at www.heinemann.co.uk/library to browse our catalogue and order online.

First published in Great Britain by Heinemann Library, Halley Court, Jordan Hill, Oxford OX2 8EJ, part of Harcourt Education. Heinemann is a registered trademark of Harcourt Education Ltd.

Editorial: Nancy Dickmann and Sarah Chappelow
Design: Ron Kamen and edesign
Illustrations: Martin Sanders
Picture Research: Maria Joannou and Christine Martin
Production: Camilla Crask

Originated by Modern Age
Printed and bound in Italy by Printer Trento srl

ISBN 0 431 19064 X
10 09 08 07 06
10 9 8 7 6 5 4 3 2 1

British Library Cataloguing in Publication Data
Spilsbury, Louise and Richard
Watching Lions in Africa. – (Wild world)
599.7'5717
A full catalogue record for this book is available from the British Library.

Acknowledgements
Alamy Images pp. **4** (Mike Hill), **7** (Chris Fredriksson), **18** (Mike Hill), **19** (Steve Bloom Pictures), **24** (Images of Africa Photobank); Ardea pp. **5** (Francois Gohier), **9** (Yann Arthus Bertrand), **11** (Chris Harvey), **16** (Ferrero-Labat), **23** (Chris Harvey), **25** (Chris Knights), **26** (Chris Harvey); Corbis pp. **10**, **15** (DiMaggio, Kalish), **20** (Fritz Polking), **27** (W. Perry Conway), **28** (Philip Perry), **29** (Kevin Schafer); FLPA p. **21** (Colin Elsey); Getty Images p. **14**; Nature PL p. **17** (Anup Shah); NHPA pp. **8** (Ann & Steve Toon), **22** (Jonathan & Angela Scott); PhotoLibrary.com p. **13** (Tim Jackson); Still Pictures p. **12** (Martin Harvey). Cover photograph of lions reproduced with permission of FLPA/Fritz Polking.

The publishers would like to thank Michael Bright of the BBC Natural History Unit for his assistance in the preparation of this book.

Contents

Words written in bold, **like this**, are explained in the glossary.

Meet the lions

This is Africa, the home of lions. Lions are some of the biggest cats in the world. They are called "king of the animals" because they are so big and strong.

Africa is the place to come to if you want to watch lions.

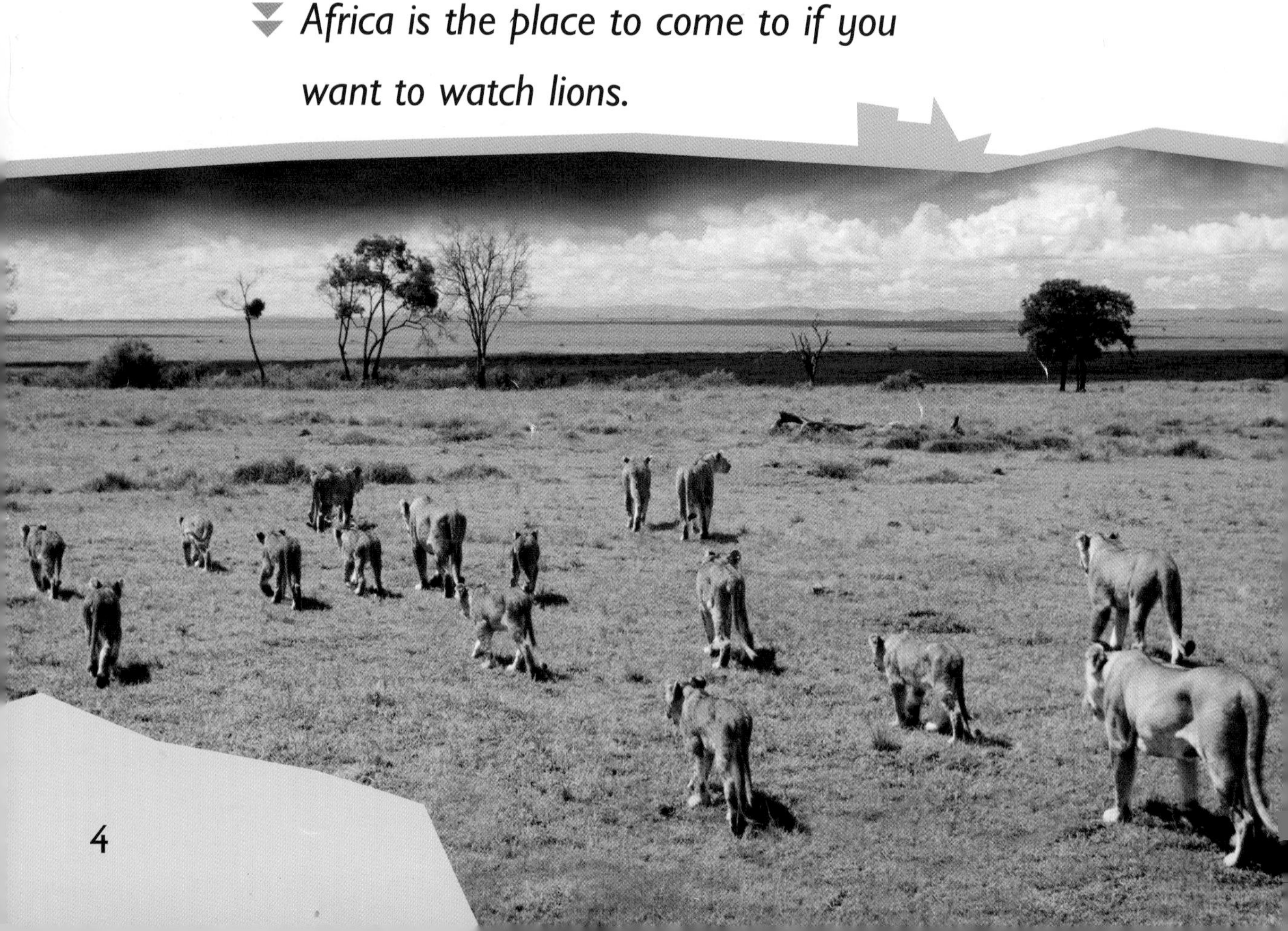

Lions are dangerous. Do not get too close!

Lions are the top **predators** in Africa. They hunt and eat many kinds of animal. No other animal will hunt a healthy adult lion.

Africa s wide open spaces

Africa is the second largest **continent** in the world. Most lions live there. There are some Asian lions in a national park in India. They look very similar to African lions.

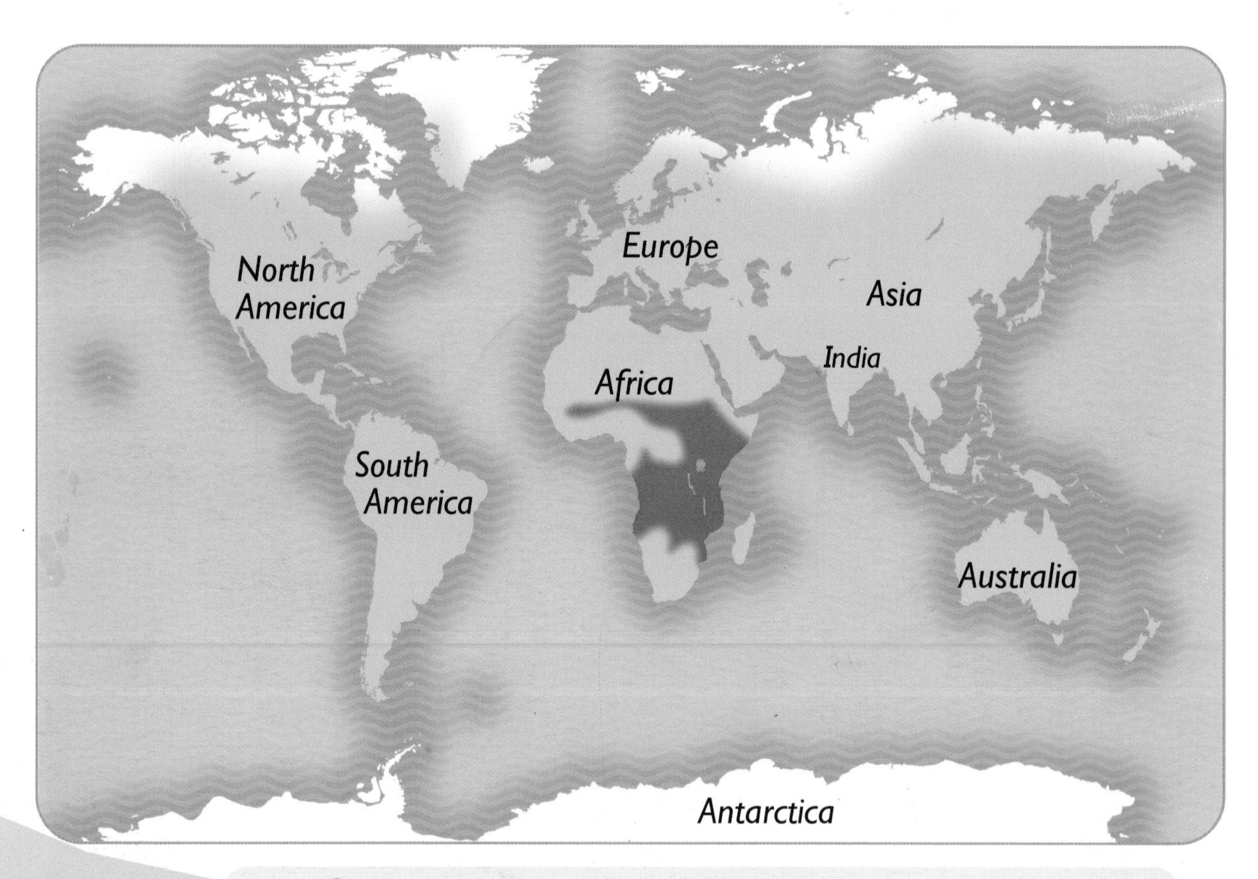

Key ● This colour shows where lions live in Africa and India.

There are lots of different kinds of land in Africa. Lions live mainly in **savannahs**. These are wide open spaces covered in grass. There are some trees and bushes.

Almost half the continent of Africa is covered in savannah like this.

There's a lion!

It is not always easy to spot lions on the **savannah**. A lion's fur is the same colour as the dry, brown grasses.

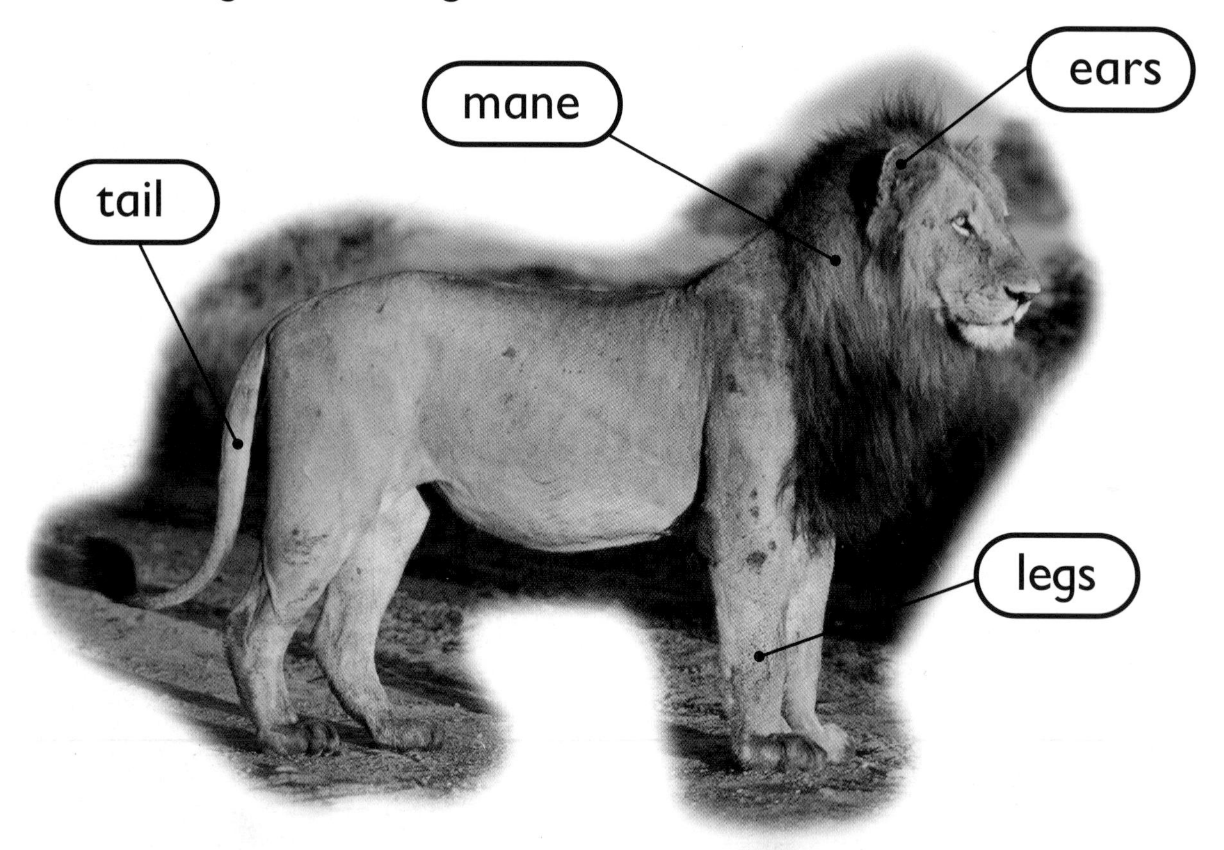

A male lion has a thick collar of fur around its neck called a mane.

This lion with two cubs is a **female**. Females are smaller than the **males** and do not have a mane. Male lions can be as long as a small car.

All lions are a sandy-brown colour.

Land of the lions

The **savannah** has huge areas of grass. Zebra, **wildebeest**, and many other animals come here to **graze**. The lions hunt and eat these animals.

Grass-eating animals such as these zebra live in big groups called ***herds****.*

The weather is hot and dry for half the year. During the dry season, it hardly ever rains. Lions often live near a **watering hole**.

This watering hole has water that the lions can drink almost all year round.

Seasons in Africa

Africa has two seasons. In the wet season lots of rain falls. The rain makes lush green grass grow. Many **herd** animals have their young at this time.

Lions often chase young animals. Young gazelles cannot run as fast as adults.

*After the big animals leave, lions must hunt other **prey**.*

Africa's hot, dry season lasts four or five months. At the end of the dry season, the grass is dried up. Many of the big **grazing** animals leave to find green grass.

A pride of lions

Lions live together in big groups, or **prides**. Each pride lives and stays in one part of the **savannah**. This is called their **territory**.

This pride has a mixture of males, females, young lions, and cubs.

The **male** lions are off on their own. It is their job to protect the **females** and the cubs. They roar loudly to tell other lions to keep off the pride's territory.

You can hear the sound of a lion's mighty roar from far away.

Lazy lions

At midday, the Sun is high in the sky and it is very hot. The lions rest. Most of them sleep in the shade of trees or rocks.

Lions spend most of the day resting.

Some of the lions **groom** each other's fur. This makes all the lions in the **pride** smell similar. They can recognize each other by smell, even at night.

This young lion looks as if it enjoys being groomed.

Lions go hunting

In the evenings, the **female** lions go hunting. They travel until they spot a **herd** of **grazing** animals. The lions sneak up on their **prey**.

If its prey looks up, the lion will freeze. It is hard to see a lion standing still in the grass.

As the lions get close to the herd, they pick out one animal to chase. They spread out and surround it. The females work together as a team.

By working together these lions can catch animals much bigger than themselves, such as this buffalo.

Feeding time

When the **female** lions catch an animal, they grab it with their sharp teeth and big claws. They are lucky if they catch their **prey**. Most lion hunts fail.

Lions must be strong and powerful to bring down a buffalo like this.

The **males** usually follow the hunt. They get to eat first. Then the females join them. The cubs usually have to wait until last for their turn.

After this big meal the lions will not need to eat again for two or three days.

Lion cubs

This **female** lion has had three cubs. Lions are **mammals**. The young cubs feed on milk from their mother's body.

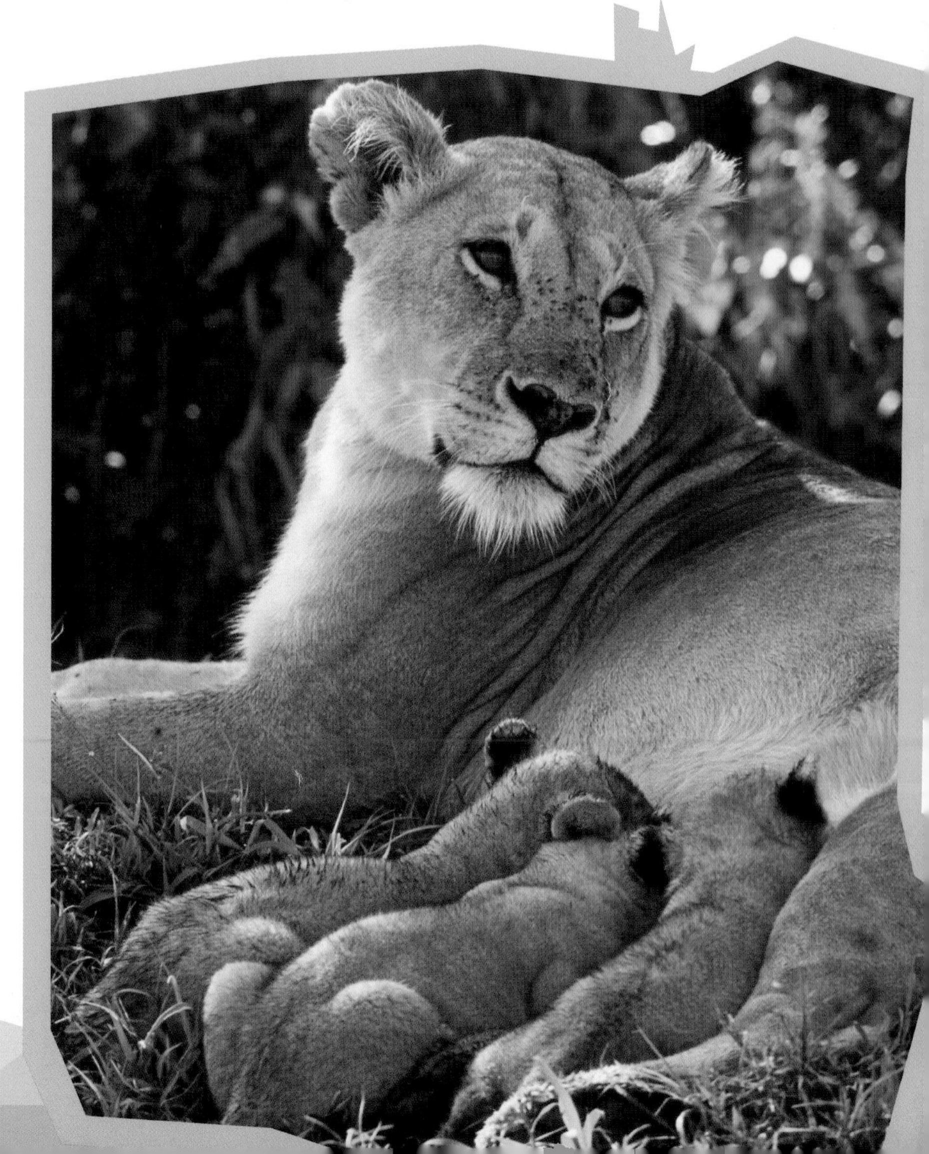

These cubs and their mother are in a safe, hidden spot.

Feeding time is over, and the mother lion is on the move. She carries the cubs to a new hiding place. Animals such as **hyenas** would eat the cubs if they found them.

It looks uncomfortable, but this mother lion is carrying her cub very gently.

Growing up

The older cubs play and fight together. This helps them learn to use their claws and teeth. It gets them ready for when they will have to fight and hunt for real.

As they play, these cubs are learning to bite, kick, and pounce on ***prey****.*

In the early evening, the cubs follow their mother on a hunting trip. She is showing them how to hunt and to find their way around the **territory**.

When this cub is about a year old it will start to catch its own prey.

Dangers

Adult lions are the top **predators** in the **savannah**, but they do face some dangers. Zebras can hurt lions by kicking them during a hunt.

When young male lions fight they can be badly hurt or even killed.

People are the biggest danger to lions. They kill lions to protect their farm animals.

Cubs are in danger from leopards and **hyenas**. Even **male** lions from outside the **pride** kill cubs. The cubs that do **survive** could have cubs of their own in a few years.

Tracker's guide

When you want to watch animals in the wild, you need to find them first. You can look for clues they leave behind.

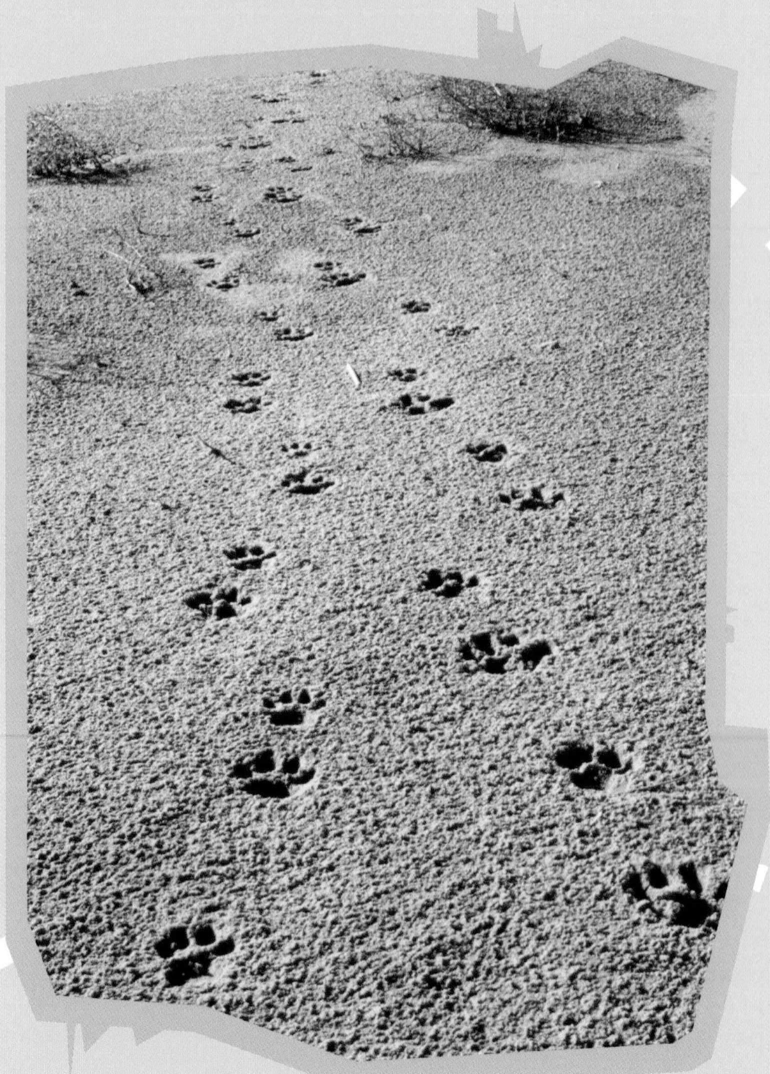

A lion's paw print looks like a very big cat's!

Lions scratch marks on to trees or land, like a cat scratches a carpet.

Lions leave dung that trackers can spot.

Glossary

continent the world is split into seven large areas of land called continents. Each continent is divided into different countries.

female animal that can become a mother when it is grown up. Girls and women are female people.

graze eat grass

groom lick and clean fur

herd group of large grass-eating animals

hyena animal, like a dog, that lives on the savannah

male animal that can become a father when it is grown up. Boys and men are male people.

mammal group of animals that feed their babies their own milk and have some hair on their bodies

predator animal that catches and eats other animals for food

prey animal that gets caught and eaten by other animals

pride group of lions

savannah area of land covered mostly in sandy soil and grass, with some trees and bushes

survive stay alive

territory area where an animal lives and feeds

watering hole pool where animals go to drink water

wildebeest kind of large animal with a big head that looks like an ox. A wildebeest is also known as a gnu.

Find out more

Books

Continents: Africa, M. Fox (Heinemann Library, 2002)

Life in a pride: Lions, Louise and Richard Spilsbury (Heinemann Library, 2004)

We're from Kenya, Vic Parker (Heinemann Library, 2005)

Why am I a mammal? Greg Pyers (Raintree, 2005)

Why do animals have paws and claws? Elizabeth Miles (Heinemann Library, 2002)

Websites

Have a look at this website to find out more exciting facts about lions:
http://www.petsandvets.com/lionfacts.htm

Find out more information about lions and where they live at this website:
http://www.nationalgeographic.com/kids/creature_feature/0109/lions2.html

Index